# DO NOT LOSE HEART
## WE WERE MADE FOR THESE TIMES

♥

compiled by Kathryn & Ross Petras

— Off the Wall Books —

copyright © 2020 Kathryn & Ross Petras

All rights reserved. No portion of this book may be reproduced — mechanically, electronically, or by any other means without written permission of the publisher.

ISBN 978-0-9904693-5-3

published by Off the Wall Books

Printed in the United States of America

First printing November 2020

# Introduction

We were finishing writing another book — a great way to keep the events outside away from our minds — and in the process, almost inadvertently (and maybe because we really needed to) we started collecting quotes which we encountered in our reading that truly, deeply comforted us.

Often it was almost as if someone was talking to us, whispering in our ears, encouraging us, telling us not to worry, convincing us that everything was going to somehow work out. Some of the quotes were so beautiful they just started, well, *singing*.

They all helped inspire, comfort, motivate, and fortify us during our own tough times.

These thoughts have the power to remind each and every one of us that we can make it through the darkness — any darkness, any time and anywhere — and emerge into the light of better times. They come from a wide range of sources,, from the ancient to the contemporary, from actors and singers to philosophers and poets, from people who have one thing in common despite their diverse backgrounds — they've experienced despair, tough times, sorrows and fears and have come through to the light.

These were the words we needed to realize we could make it through it all. We hope they do the same for you. Stay strong!

—Kathy & Ross

Do not lose hope — what you seek will be found. Trust ghosts. Trust those that you have helped to help you in their turn. Trust dreams. Trust your heart, and trust your story.

—Neil Gaiman
*writer*

Hey you, keep living. It won't always be this overwhelming.

—Jacqueline Whitney
*poet*

In the middle of winter I at last discovered that there was in me an invincible summer.

—Albert Camus
*philosopher*

The world, you see, is happier after the terror of the storm ... you have noticed that truth comes into this world with two faces. One is sad with suffering, and the other laughs; but it is the same face, laughing or weeping.

—Black Elk
*Wichasha Wakan*

Don't be afraid to excuse yourself. Recharge for as long as you need. Lean up against a tree and take a break from the other bears. I'll be there too, but I promise not to bother you.

—Amy Schumer
*comedian*

I was okay just a moment ago. I will learn how to be okay again.

—Nina LaCour
*writer*

# You can fall, but you can rise also.

—Angelique Kidjo
*singer/songwriter*

You can do hard things. You will get through, you will make a decision and one day you will look back and think, "Remember when?"

—Rachel Marie Martin
*writer*

I too, have felt despair many times in my life, but I do not keep a chair for it. I will not entertain it. It is not allowed to eat from my plate.

—Clarissa Pinkola Estés
*writer*

# In life you control what you can.

—Michelle Obama
*attorney*

Pain is inevitable. Suffering is optional.

—Haruki Murakami
*writer*

All human life has its seasons, and no one's personal chaos can be permanent: winter, after all, does not last forever, does it? There is summer, too, and spring, and though sometimes when branches stay dark and the Earth cracks with ice, one thinks they will never come, that spring, that summer, but they do, and always.

—Truman Capote
*writer*

Don't be defined by what you're losing during this crisis, but by how you respond to it.

—Malala Yousafzai
*activist*

Nothing happens to people that they are not formed by nature to bear.

—Marcus Aurelius
*philosopher/emperor*

There is nothing in the world, I venture to say, that would so effectively help one to survive even the worst conditions, as the knowledge that there is a meaning in one's life.

—Viktor Frankl
*psychiatrist*

# In a time of destruction, create something.

—Maxine Hong Kingston
*writer*

Nothing is worth more than laughter. It is strength to laugh and to abandon oneself, to be light. Tragedy is the most ridiculous thing.

—Frida Kahlo
*artist*

In times of stress, the best thing we can do for each other is to listen with our ears and our hearts and to be assured that our questions are just as important as our answers.

—Fred Rogers
*children's television host*

It is impossible for you to go on as you were before, so you must go on as you never have.

—Cheryl Strayed
*writer*

Laughter isn't even the other side of tears. It is tears turned inside out. Truly the suffering is great, here on earth. We blunder along, shredded by our mistakes, bludgeoned by our faults. Not having a clue where the dark path leads us. But on the whole, we stumble along bravely, don't you think?

—Alice Walker
*writer*

When we are stricken and cannot bear our lives any longer, then a tree has something to say to us: Be still! Be still! Look at me! Life is not easy, life is not difficult. Those are childish thoughts . . .

—Herman Hesse
*writer*

# Don't fear difficult moments. The best comes from them.

—Rita Levi-Montalcini
*neurobiologist*

# No one is ever safe. So why not live as much as you can?

—Rita Mae Brown
*writer*

I took a deep breath and listened to the old brag of my heart: I am, I am, I am.

—Sylvia Plath
*writer*

Things happen to you. But they don't have to happen to your soul.

—Jennifer Lawrence
*actor*

When you get to the end of all the light you know and it's time to step into the darkness of the unknown, faith is knowing that one of two things shall happen: either you will be given something solid to stand on, or you will be taught how to fly.

—Edward Teller
*physicist*

When we look at our lives as a whole, our current difficulty is like a cloud. Although large, it will soon pass.

—Haemin Sunim
*monk*

The very least you can do in your life is figure out what you hope for. And the most you can do is live inside that hope. Not admire it from a distance but live right in it, under its roof.

—Barbara Kingsolver
*writer*

Deep within every crisis is an opportunity for something beautiful.

—Kate McGahan
*counselor/writer*

Be patient and tough; someday this pain will be useful to you.

—Ovid
*poet*

# What would you do if you weren't afraid?

—Sheryl Sandberg
*business executive/philanthropist*

Courage is like — it's a habit, a virtue: you get it by courageous acts. It's like you learn to swim by swimming. You learn courage by couraging.

—Marie Daly
*chemist*

Facing it, always facing it, that's the way to get through. Face it.

—Joseph Conrad
*writer*

there is light somewhere.
it may not be much light but
it beats the darkness.

>—Charles Bukowski
> *writer*

The two best prayers I know are "Help me, help me," and "Thank you, thank you."

—Anne Lamott
*writer*

There is no courage without vulnerability. I don't want you to be vulnerable and all gooey for vulnerability's sake. I hate that crap. That is not my personality at all. I'm just saying that vulnerability is the birthplace of courage. And if we want to be brave, we have to be real. And that requires risk.

—Brené Brown
*social work professor*

Pretend that this is a time of miracles and we believe in them.

—Edwidge Danticat
*writer*

Some days are way worse, some days aren't. But you know what I can do? I can go, "Well, my hands work; my arms work; my legs work, even though they are sore; my back works; my brain works; my heart works; I'm taking breaths, my lungs work." You can just be grateful for what you can do.

—Lady Gaga
*singer*

God never slams
a door in your
face without
opening a box of
Girl Scout
cookies . . .

—Elizabeth Gilbert
*writer*

That glimmer of light, surrounded by so many shadows, seemed to say without words: Evil has not yet taken complete dominion. A spark of hope is still left.

—Isaac Bashevis Singer
*writer*

Be comforted, dear soul! There is always light behind the clouds.

—Louisa May Alcott
*writer*

# Courage is only an accumulation of small steps.

—György Konrád
*politician*

Should you shield the valleys from the windstorms, you would never see the beauty of their canyons.

—Elisabeth Kübler-Ross
*physician*

Those who are unaware they are walking in darkness will never seek the light.

—Bruce Lee
*martial arts fighter*

Anything scares any one but really after all considering how dangerous everything is nothing is really very frightening.

—Gertrude Stein
*writer*

I am still encouraged to go on. I wouldn't know where else to go.

—E.B. White
*writer*

Break a vase, and the love that reassembles the fragments is stronger than that love which took its symmetry for granted when it was whole.

—Derek Walcott
*poet*

Some of you young folks been saying to me, "Hey Pops, what you mean 'What a wonderful world?' How about all them wars all over the place? You call them wonderful? And how about hunger and pollution? That ain't so wonderful either." Well how about listening to old Pops for a minute. Seems to me, it ain't the world that's so bad but what we're doin' to it. And all I'm saying is, see, what a wonderful world it would be if only we'd give it a chance. Love, baby, love. That's the secret, yeah. If lots more of us loved each other, we'd solve lots more problems. And then this world would be better. That's what ol' Pops keeps saying.

—Louis Armstrong
*musician*

stay strong
through your
pain
grow flowers
from it

—Rupi Kaur
*poet*

In three words I can sum up everything I've learned about life: it goes on.

—Robert Frost
poet

In times of crisis, it's wonderful what the imagination will do.

—Ruskin Bond
*writer*

To experience the good you have to have seen the bad; plus it makes you appreciate blessings more.

—Pink
*singer*

And one has to understand that braveness is not the absence of fear but rather the strength to keep on going forward despite the fear.

—Paulo Coelho
*writer*

I don't think of
all the misery
but of the
beauty that still
remains.

—Anne Frank
*diarist*

Now that I knew fear, I also knew it was not permanent. As powerful as it was, its grip on me would loosen. It would pass.

—Louise Erdrich
*writer*

If the sky falls
they shall
have clouds
for supper.

—Charles Simic
*poet*

There are days I drop words of comfort on myself like falling leaves and remember that it is enough to be taken care of by myself.

—Brian Andreas
*writer*

The present is the ever moving shadow that divides yesterday from tomorrow. In that lies hope.

—Frank Lloyd Wright
*architect*

Be not afraid of life. Believe that life is worth living, and your belief will help create the fact.

—William James
*philosopher*

Not everything that is faced can be changed. But nothing can be changed until it is faced.

—James Baldwin
*writer*

A time of crisis is not just a time of anxiety and worry . It gives a chance, an opportunity, to choose well or to choose badly. You have to decide which way you want.

—Desmond Tutu
*humanitarian*

Even if happiness forgets you a little bit, never completely forget about it.

—Jacques Prevert
*poet*

It is only in our darkest hours that we may discover the true strength of the brilliant light within ourselves that can never, ever, be dimmed.

—Doe Zantamata
*artist*

# The universe is calling you to be a little bit braver.

—Elaine Welteroth
*writer*

I had forgotten that time wasn't fixed like concrete but in fact was fluid as sand, or water. I had forgotten that even misery can end.

—Joyce Carol Oates
*writer*

Say to them . . .
"even if you are
not ready for day
it cannot always
be night."
You will be right.

—Gwendolyn Brooks
poet

We are never alone. Not when the night is darkest, the wind coldest, the world seemingly most indifferent...

—Taylor Caldwell
*writer*

People say to me all the time, "You have no fear." I tell them, "No, that's not true. I'm scared all the time. You have to have fear in order to have courage. I'm a courageous person because I'm a scared person."

—Ronda Rousey
*fighter*

You may not control all the events that happen to you, but you can decide not to be reduced by them.

—Maya Angelou
*writer*

# Gray skies are just clouds passing over.

—Duke Ellington
*composer/musician*

We dream to give ourselves hope. To stop dreaming - well, that's like saying you can never change your fate.

—Amy Tan
*writer*

I think laughter may be a form of courage. As humans we sometimes stand tall and look into the sun and laugh, and I think we are never more brave than when we do that.

—Linda Ellerbee
*journalist*

Even if the present is desperately dark, I do not wish to leave it. Will tomorrow be free from darkness? We'll talk about that tomorrow.

—Lu Xun
*writer*

Think about a thunderstorm, they have a chaotic sound but when they are over everything is clean, fresh and beautiful again.

—Bob Ross
*artist*

Just keep laughing. It's all we can do.

—Judi Dench
*actor*

The news is beyond terrible right now, but don't forget, despite all your care & concern, to make a little room for your own brain in all this so you can show up to fight another day.

—Aparna Nancherla
*comedian*

It's amazing how a little tomorrow can make up for a whole lot of yesterday.

—John Guare
*playwright*

We all get scared and want to turn away, but it isn't always strength that makes you stay. Strength is also making the decision to change your destiny.

— Zoraida Córdova
*writer*

If we have our own *why* in life, we shall get along with almost any *how*.

—Friedrich Nietzsche
*philosopher*

Don't ever become a pessimist . . . a pessimist is correct oftener than an optimist, but an optimist has more fun, and neither can stop the march of events.

—Robert A. Heinlein
*writer*

There is no end. There is no beginning. There is only the infinite passion of life.

—Federico Fellini
film director

You ask what is the ultimate answer? It is the song of the fisherman, sailing back to shore.

—Wang Wei
*poet*

I must not fear.
Fear is the mind-killer.
Fear is the little-death that brings total obliteration.
I will face my fear.
I will permit it to pass over me and through me.
And when it has gone past I will turn the inner eye to see its path.
Where the fear has gone there will be nothing.
Only I will remain.

—Frank Herbert
*writer*

Watch the path of the stars, and know that you too are moving along with them.

—Marcus Aurelius
*emperor/philosopher*

Hope is important because it can make the present moment less difficult to bear. If we believe that tomorrow will be better, we can bear a hardship today.

—Thich Nhat Hanh
*spiritual leader*

Don't feel sorry for yourself. Only assholes do that.

—Haruki Murakami
*writer*

# Life offers up these moments of joy despite everything.

—Sally Rooney
*writer*

When I was a boy and I would see scary things in the news, my mother would say to me, "Look for the helpers. You will always find people who are helping." To this day, especially in times of "disaster," I remember my mother's words, and I am always comforted by realizing that there are still so many helpers — so many caring people in this world.

—Fred Rogers
*children's tv host*

If you surrender to the wind you can ride it.

—Toni Morrison
*writer*

Sometimes you have to let go of the picture of what you thought life would be like and learn to find joy in the story you are actually living.

—Rachel Marie Martin
*writer*

# Sometimes all that is necessary is for you to wait.

—Nanea Hoffman
*writer*

Our greatest problems in life come not so much from the situations we confront as from our doubts about our ability to handle them.

—Susan L. Taylor
*editor*

Try to exclude the possibility of suffering which the order of nature and the existence of free wills involve, and you find that you have excluded life itself.

—C.S. Lewis
scholar/writer

Things could always be better, but things could always be worse.

—Marla Gibbs
*actor*

People who have struggled constantly with problems become hardened through suffering; and don't give in. And even if they fall, they still fight on their knees.

—Seneca the Younger
*philosopher*

There are opportunities even in the most difficult moments.

—Wangari Maathai
*writer*

However mean your life is, meet it and live it; do not shun it and call it hard names. It is not so bad as you are. It looks poorest when you are richest. The fault-finder will find faults even in paradise. Love your life, poor as it is. You may perhaps have some pleasant, thrilling, glorious hours, even in a poorhouse. The setting sun is reflected from the windows of the almshouse as brightly as from the rich man's abode; the snow melts before its door as early in the spring. I do not see but a quiet mind may live as contentedly there, and have as cheering thoughts, as in a palace.

—Henry David Thoreau
*writer*

Man, when you lose your laugh you lose your footing.

—Ken Kesey
*writer*

The dark does not weep for itself because there is no light. Rather, it accepts that it is the dark. It is said that even the gods must die . . . But not without one hell of a fight.

—Libba Bray
*writer*

Diamonds are created from intense pressure over long periods of time; pearls are formed around irritants. Precious things are made from discomfort.

—Maggie Smith
*poet*

You never know how strong you are until being strong is your only choice.

—Bob Marley
*singer/songwriter*

[T]here is nothing so great as to be capable of happiness; to pluck it out of "each moment and whatever happens"; to find that one can ride as gay and buoyant on the angry, menacing, tumultuous waves of life as on those that glide and glitter under a clear sky; that it is not defeat and wretchedness which come out of the storm of adversity, but strength and calmness.

—Anne Gilchrist
*writer*

Nothing in life is to be feared, it is only to be understood. Now is the time to understand more, so that we may fear less.

—Marie Curie
*physicist/chemist*

You may trod me in the very dirt
But still, like dust, I'll rise.

—Maya Angelou
*writer*

Life isn't about waiting for the storm to pass. It's about learning how to dance in the rain.

—Vivian Greene
*writer*

Bad times are good times to prepare for better times.

—Ruskin Bond
*writer*

There will be times when standing alone feels too hard, too scary, and we'll doubt our ability to make our way through the uncertainty. Someone, somewhere, will say, "Don't do it. You don't have what it takes to survive the wilderness." This is when you reach deep into your wild heart and remind yourself, "I am the wilderness."

—Brené Brown
*social work professor*

I promise you nothing is as chaotic as it seems.

—Steve Maraboli
*writer*

Times of crisis, of disruption or constructive change, are not only predictable, but desirable. They mean growth.

—Fyodor Dostoevsky
*writer*

Barn's burnt down, now I can see the moon.

—Mizuta Masahide
*poet*

Patience is a form of wisdom. It demonstrates that we understand and accept the fact that sometimes things must unfold in their own time.

—Jon Kabat-Zinn
*teacher*

To those who've survived: Breathe. That's it. Once more. Good. You're good. Even if you're not, you're alive. That is a victory.

—N.K. Jemisin
*writer*

Whatever the present moment contains, accept it as if you had chosen it. Always work with it, not against it. Make it your friend and ally, not your enemy.

—Eckhart Tolle
*teacher*

When it comes to your life, you are not just the artist, but the masterpiece as well.

—Cleo Wade
*poet*

To be hopeful in bad times is not just foolishly romantic. It is based on the fact that human history is a history not only of cruelty, but also of compassion, sacrifice, courage, kindness. What we choose to emphasize in this complex history will determine our lives. If we see only the worst, it destroys our capacity to do something. If we remember those times and places — and there are so many — where people have behaved magnificently, this gives us the energy to act, and at least the possibility of sending this spinning top of a world in a different direction. And if we do act, in however small a way, we don't have to wait for some grand utopian future. The future is an infinite succession of presents, and to live now as we think human beings should live, in defiance of all that is bad around us, is itself a marvelous victory.

—Howard Zinn
*historian*

There is always a little more toothpaste in the tube. Think about it.

—Bill Bryson
*writer*

Right in the difficult we must have our joys, our happiness, our dreams: there against the depth of this background, they stand out, there for the first time we see how beautiful they are.

—Rainer Maria Rilke
*poet*

Sorrow eats time.
Be patient.
Time eats sorrow.

—Louise Erdrich
*writer*

Hope begins in the dark, the stubborn hope that if you just show up and try to do the right thing, the dawn will come. You wait and watch and work: you don't give up.

—Anne Lamott
*writer*

If you remain calm in the midst of great chaos, it is the surest guarantee that it will eventually subside.

—Julie Andrews
*actor*

The world is violent and mercurial — it will have its way with you. We are saved only by love — love for each other and the love that we pour into the art we feel compelled to share: being a parent; being a writer; being a painter; being a friend. We live in a perpetually burning building, and what we must save from it, all the time, is love.

—Tennessee Williams
*playwright*

It's funny how, when things seem the darkest, moments of beauty present themselves in the most unexpected places.

—Karen Marie Moning
*writer*

At the end of the day, we can endure much more than we think we can.

—Frida Kahlo
*artist*

The world breaks everyone and afterward many are strong at the broken places.

—Ernest Hemingway
*writer*

We have two lives . . . the life we learn with and the life we live after that. Suffering is what brings us towards happiness.

—Bernard Malamud
*writer*

Hope is being able to see that there is light despite all of the darkness.

—Desmond Tutu
*humanitarian*

Rabbit said: "I'm afraid."
"What are you afraid of?" asked his friend, Bear.
"I don't know," said Rabbit. "I just am."
"Then, I will sit with you until you're not afraid any more," said Bear. "We will face it together."

—Tara Shannon
*artist/writer*

And I get up because it is the only thing I can do.

—Jessamyn Ward
*writer*

Most things will be okay eventually, but not everything will be. Sometimes you'll put up a good fight and lose. Sometimes you'll hold on really hard and realize there is no choice but to let go. Acceptance is a small, quiet room.

—Cheryl Strayed
*writer*

Just when you think it can't get any worse, it can. And just when you think it can't get any better, it can.

—Nicholas Sparks
*writer*

Here is the world.
Beautiful and
terrible things
will happen.
Don't be afraid.

—Frederick Buechner
*theologian*

Wherever you are tonight, you can make it. Hold your head high, stick your chest out. You can make it. It gets dark sometimes, but the morning comes. Don't you surrender. Suffering breeds character, character breeds faith. In the end faith will not disappoint. You must not surrender.

—Jesse Jackson
*activist*

# Be happy for this moment.

—Omar Khayyam
*poet*

Do not give way to useless alarm; though it is right to be prepared for the worst, there is no occasion to look on it as certain.

—Jane Austen
*writer*

# Grief and resilience live together.

—Michelle Obama
*attorney*

One discovers the light in the darkness, that is what darkness is for; but everything in our lives depends on how we bear the light. It is necessary, while in darkness, to know that there is a light somewhere, to know that in oneself, waiting to be found, there is a light. What the light reveals is danger, and what it demands is faith.

—James Baldwin
*writer*

Though we tremble before uncertain futures, may we meet illness, death and adversity with strength. May we dance in the face of our fears.

—Gloria Anzaldúa
*scholar*

You need the dark in order to show the light.

—Bob Ross
*artist*

You have to temper the iron. Every hardship is an opportunity that you are given, an opportunity to grow. To grow is the sole purpose of existence on this planet Earth. You will not grow if you sit in a beautiful flower garden, but you will grow if you are sick, if you are in pain, if you experience losses, and if you do not put your head in the sand, but take the pain as a gift to you with a very, very specific purpose.

—Elisabeth Kübler-Ross
*physician*

It's never too late while you're breathing.

—Lois McMaster Bujold
*writer*

Everything passes away — suffering, pain, blood, hunger, pestilence. The sword will pass away too, but the stars will still remain when the shadows of our presence and our deeds have vanished from the earth. There is no man who does not know that. Why, then, will we not turn our eyes towards the stars? Why?

—Mikhail Bulgakov
*writer*

No matter how much falls on us, we keep plowing ahead. That's the only way to keep the roads clear.

—Greg Kincaid
*writer*

What lies behind you and what lies in front of you, pales in comparison to what lies inside of you.

—Ralph Waldo Emerson
*essayist/philosopher*

Normal has a way of returning. It will ebb and flow and we will push and try but then, one day, there it will be. Normal. This is the time when you get to explore, get to be brave, get to write the new normal.

—Rachel Marie Martin
*writer*

Thanks for this day, for all birds safe in their nests, for whatever this is, for life.

—Barbara Kingsolver
*writer*

That is one good thing about this world . . . there are always sure to be more springs.

—L.M. Montgomery
*writer*

On the road, they have these LG televisions and when you turn them on, it says: Life Is Good. I love that, Actually, I say it out loud when I turn it on: "Life is good." Because there's a million reasons why we can say that things are terrible in the world, but when you get down to it, you know, being alive, I mean, it's the best thing we got.

—Patti Smith
*musician/writer*

Courage doesn't always roar. Sometimes courage is the little voice at the end of the day that says "I'll try again tomorrow."

—Mary Anne Radmacher
*writer*

As you proceed through life following your own path, birds will sh*t on you. Don't bother to brush it off. Getting a comedic view of your situation gives you spiritual distance. Having a sense of humor saves you.

—Joseph Campbell,
*mythologist*

Whether it's the best of times or the worst of times, it's the only time we've got.

—Art Buchwald
*humorist*

The world just happens to you sometimes, is what I think. And people just gotta keep moving through it, best they can.

—Elizabeth Gilbert
*writer*

All shall be well, and all shall be well, and all manner of things shall be well.

—Julian of Norwich
*mystic*

Happiness isn't something that depends on our surroundings . . . it's something we make inside ourselves.

—Corrie Ten Boom
*activist*

Although the world is full of suffering, it is also full of the overcoming of it.

—Helen Keller
*humanitarian*

Be scared. You can't help that. But don't be afraid. Ain't nothing in the woods going to hurt you unless you corner it, or it smells that you are afraid. A bear or a deer, too, has got to be scared of a coward the same as a brave man has got to be.

—William Faulkner
*writer*

Either life entails courage, or it ceases to be life.

—E.M. Forster
*writer*

Fear is real and there is nothing you can do about it except to keep functioning, keep your hands and legs and body moving, your mind focused on the task at hand.

—Alvah Bessie
*writer*

# Live through it ... That's all we can do.

—Larry McMurtry
*writer*

You can't laugh and be afraid at the same time — of anything. If you're laughing, I defy you to be afraid.

—Stephen Colbert
*comedian*

*Cowardly Lion*: Courage! What makes a king out of a slave? Courage! What makes the flag on the mast to wave? Courage! What makes the elephant charge his tusk in the misty mist, or the dusky dusk? What makes the muskrat guard his musk? Courage! What makes the sphinx the seventh wonder? Courage! What makes the dawn come up like thunder? Courage! What makes the

Hottentot so hot? What puts the "ape" in apricot? What have they got that I ain't got? *Dorothy, Scarecrow, Tin Woodsman*: Courage! *Cowardly Lion*: You can say that again! Hunh!

—Yip Harburg
*screenwriter*
in the film The Wizard of Oz *(1939)*

I learned that courage was not the absence of fear, but the triumph over it. The brave man is not he who does not feel afraid, but he who conquers that fear.

—Nelson Mandela
*statesman*

We are all in the gutter, but some of us are looking at the stars.

—Oscar Wilde
*writer*

Most people live, whether physically, intellectually or morally, in a very restricted circle of their potential being. They make use of a very small portion of their possible consciousness, and of their soul's resources in general, much like a man who, out of his whole bodily organism, should get into a habit of using and moving only his little finger. Great emergencies and crises show us how much greater our vital resources are than we had supposed.

—William James
*psychologist*

There is no mountain that cannot be climbed and there are more pathways to the top than we could ever imagine.

—Cleo Wade
*poet*

Despair is only for those who see the end beyond all doubt. We do not.

—J.R.R. Tolkien
*writer*

The sea rises, the light fails, lovers cling to each other, and children cling to us. The moment we cease to hold each other, the moment we break faith with one another, the sea engulfs us and the light goes out.

—James Baldwin
*writer*

# Fire tries gold, misfortune tries the brave.

—Seneca the Younger
*philosopher*

If there is a meaning in life at all, then there must be a meaning in suffering. Suffering is an ineradicable part of life, even as fate and death.

—Victor Frankl
*psychiatrist*

One of the hardest things to make a child understand is, that down underneath your feet, if you go far enough, you come to blue sky and stars again; that there really is no "down" for the world, but only in every direction an "up."

—Anne Gilchrist
*writer*

Miracles happen all the time. We're here, aren't we?

—Marilyn Nelson
*poet*

The dark does not destroy the light; it defines it. It's our fear of the dark that casts our joy into the shadows.

—Brené Brown
*social work professor*

Boredom, anger, sadness, or fear are not "yours," not personal. They are conditions of the human mind. They come and go. Nothing that comes and goes is you.

—Eckhart Tolle
*teacher*

Even the worst days have an ending, and the best days have a beginning.

—Jennifer Coletta
*writer*

There is evidence of bad sh*t having been survived before. Ancient Advice Left in cave by Wise French Caveman: "When Bigbad Sh*t come, no run scream hide. Try paint picture of it on wall. Drum to it. Sing to it. Dance to it. This give you handle on it."

—Ken Kesey
*writer*

I am not afraid of storms, for I am learning how to sail my ship.

—Louisa May Alcott
*writer*

She decided long ago that life was a long journey. She would be strong, and she would be weak, and both would be okay.

—Tahereh Mafi
*writer*

Hoping for the best, prepared for the worst, and unsurprised by anything in between.

—Maya Angelou
*writer*

Be like a promontory against which the waves are always breaking. It stands fast, and stills the waters that rage around it.

—Marcus Aurelius
*philosopher/emperor*

# Even the darkest night will end and the sun will rise.

—Victor Hugo
*writer*

Hope is a renewable option: If you run out of it at the end of the day, you get to start over in the morning.

—Barbara Kingsolver
*writer*

How can you make peace with what is? That's the recipe for happiness.

—Haemin Sunim
*monk*

if you were born with
the weakness to fall
you were born with
the strength to rise

—Rupi Kaur
*poet*

In the external scheme of things, shining moments are as brief as the twinkling of an eye, yet such twinklings are what eternity is made of -- moments when we human beings can say "I love you," "I'm proud of you," "I forgive you," "I'm grateful for you." That's what eternity is made of: invisible imperishable good stuff.

—Fred Rogers
*children's tv host*

I am the one thing in life I can control.

—Lin-Manuel Miranda
*writer*

You have done enough.
You are enough.
You were born enough.
The world is waiting on
you.

—Elaine Welteroth<br>
*writer*

I can be miserable if I want to. You don't need to try and make it go away. It shouldn't go away. It's just as sad as it ought to be and I'm not going to hide from what's true just because it hurts.

—Toni Morrison
*writer*

# The more you feel, the stronger you are.

—Alice Hoffman
*writer*

# It is your reaction to difficulties that show what you are.

—Epictetus
*philosopher*

You can cut all the flowers but you cannot keep Spring from coming.

—Pablo Neruda
*poet*

Sometimes fate is like a small sandstorm that keeps changing directions. You change direction but the sandstorm chases you. . . . This storm is you. Something inside of you. So all you can do is give in to it, step right inside the storm, closing your eyes and plugging up your ears so the sand doesn't get in, and walk through it, step by step. There's no sun there, no moon, no direction, no sense of time. Just fine white sand swirling up into the sky like pulverized bones.

That's the kind of sandstorm you need to imagine.
And you really will have to make it through that violent, metaphysical, symbolic storm.

>—Haruki Murakami
>*writer*

If I can't make it through one door, I'll go through another door—or I'll make a door. Something terrific will come no matter how dark the present.

—Joan Rivers
*comedian*

Just because I made it here doesn't mean it was easy. And just because I don't seem overwhelmed doesn't mean I'm not.

—Jen Wilde
*writer*

I know not all that may be coming, but be it what it will, I'll go to it laughing.

—Herman Melville
*writer*

Your responses to the events of life are more important than the events themselves.

—Virginia Satir
*therapist*

There is light in darkness, you just have to find it.

—bell hooks
*poet*

Self-pity is a dead-end road. You make the choice to drive down it. It's up to you to decide to stay parked there or to turn around and drive out.

—Cheryl Strayed
*writer*

> You have come to the shore. There are no instructions.
>
> —Denise Levertov
> *poet*

# Don't be afraid to be afraid.

—Madeleine L'Engle
*writer*

Lie down for ten minutes and just breathe. Unplug from the chaos of life long enough to connect with whatever calms you. Claim the time it takes to be happy.

—Martha Beck
*writer*

And I tell myself: a moon will rise from my darkness.

—Mahmoud Darwish
*poet*

I'm not saying that everything is survivable. Just that everything except the last thing is.

—John Green
*writer*

Man is fond of counting his troubles, but he does not count his joys. If he counted them up as he ought to, he would see that every lot has enough happiness provided for it.

—Fyodor Dostoevsky
*writer*

We are always more afraid than we wish to be, but we can always be braver than we expect.

—Robert Jordan
*writer*

You're only human. You don't have to have it together every minute of every day.

—Anne Hathaway
*actor*

Life is not the way it's supposed to be, it's the way it is. The way you cope with it is what makes the difference.

—Virginia Satir
*therapist*

Everything is temporary. You can't keep a white-knuckled hold on what you love or on what has hurt you. Loosen your grip on your grief today, if only a bit.

—Maggie Smith
*poet*

As long as there is still breath, there's forward.

—Oprah Winfrey
*media mogul*

The women whom I love and admire for their strength and grace did not get that way because sh*t worked out. They got that way because sh*t went wrong, and they handled it. They handled it in a thousand different ways on a thousand different days, but they handled it. Those women are my superheroes.

—Elizabeth Gilbert
*writer*

Fear is not the enemy. Waiting to stop feeling afraid is.

—Marie Forleo
*entrepreneur*

It is easy to forget that there are always as good grounds for optimism as for pessimism – exactly the same grounds, in fact . . .

—Marilynne Robinson
*writer*

There are moments when troubles enter our lives and we can do nothing to avoid them. But they are there for a reason. Only when we have overcome them will we understand why they were there.

—Paulo Coelho
*writer*

Going through challenging things can teach you a lot, and they also make you appreciate the times that aren't so challenging.

—Carrie Fisher
*actor/writer*

Depend upon it, you see but half. You see the evil, but you do not see the consolation. There will be little rubs and disappointments everywhere, and we are all apt to expect too much; but then, if one scheme of happiness fails, human nature turns to another; if the first calculation is wrong, we make a second better: we find comfort somewhere.

—Jane Austen
*writer*

As much as we want to keep ourselves safe, we can't protect ourselves from everything. If we want to embrace life, we also have to embrace chaos.

—Susan Elizabeth Phillips
*writer*

Anyone can hide. Facing up to things, working through them, that's what makes you strong.

—Sarah Dessen
*writer*

If I were asked to give what I consider the single most useful bit of advice for all humanity it would be this: Expect trouble as an inevitable part of life and when it comes, hold you head high, look it squarely in the eye and say, "I will be bigger than you. You cannot defeat me."

—Ann Landers
*advice columnist*

Sometimes you just need to breathe, trust, let go, and see what happens.

—Mandy Hale
*writer*

And whatever happens, we just need to endure . . . Which brings me to my favorite quote from a favorite novel, John Steinbeck's "The Grapes of Wrath." Ma Joad gives the family this homespun pep talk when the car breaks down on the way to California: "This here bearing went out. We didn't know it was goin', so we didn' worry none. Now she's out an' we'll fix her. An' by Christ that goes for the rest of it."

—David Allen
editor

If we were not
meant to dance,
why all this music?

—Gregory Orr
*poet*

The human capacity for burden is like bamboo — far more flexible than you'd ever believe at first glance.

—Jodi Picoult
*writer*

I believe in being strong when everything seems to be going wrong . . . I believe that tomorrow is another day and I believe in miracles.

—Audrey Hepburn
*actor*

With all its sham, drudgery and broken dreams, it is still a beautiful world. Be cheerful. Strive to be happy.

—Max Ehrmann
*writer/lawyer*

Take a shower, wash off the day. Drink a glass of water. Make the room dark. Lie down and close your eyes. Notice the silence. Notice your heart. Still beating. Still fighting. You made it, after all. You made it, another day. And you can make it one more. You're doing just fine.

—Charlotte Eriksson
*writer/singer*

Hope is the thing with feathers —
That perches in the soul —
And sings the tune without the words —
And never stops — at all —

—Emily Dickenson
*poet*

We must embrace pain and burn it as fuel for our journey.

—Kenji Miyazawa
*writer*

All is well. Everything is working out for my highest good. Out of this situation only good will come. I am safe.

—Louise Hay
*writer*

The most beautiful people we have known are those who have known defeat, known suffering, known struggle, known loss, and have found their way out of the depths. These persons have an appreciation, a sensitivity, and an understanding of life that fills them with compassion, gentleness, and a deep loving concern. Beautiful people do not just happen.

—Elisabeth Kübler-Ross
*physician*

You must learn to let go. Release the stress. You were never in control anyway.

—Steve Maraboli
*writer*

Our greatest disappointments and painful experiences —if we can make meaning out of them— can lead us toward becoming more of who we are.

—Gloria E. Anzaldúa
*scholar*

I say I'm stronger than fear.

—Malala Yousafzai
*activist*

The moments that make life worth living are when things are at their worst and you find a way to laugh.

—Amy Schumer
*comedian*

You expected to be sad in the fall. Part of you died each year when the leaves fell from the trees and their branches were bare against the wind and the cold, wintery light. But you knew there would always be the spring, as you knew the river would flow again after it was frozen.

—Ernest Hemingway
*writer*

Crying is all right in its way while it lasts. But you have to stop sooner or later, and then you still have to decide what to do.

—C.S. Lewis
*writer*

# Smile, breathe, and go slowly.

—Thích Nhat Hạnh
*monk*

Adversity is like a strong wind. I don't mean just that it holds us back from places we might otherwise go. It also tears away from us all but the things that cannot be torn, so that afterward we see ourselves as we really are, and not merely as we might like to be.

—Arthur Golden
*writer*

You don't have to control your thoughts. You just have to stop letting them control you.

—Dan Millman
*writer*

Caring for myself is not self-indulgence, it is self-preservation.

—Audre Lorde
*poet*

How great it is when we come to know that times of disappointment can be followed by joy; that guilt over falling short of our ideals can be replaced by pride in doing all that we can; and that anger can be channeled into creative achievements . . . and into dreams that we can make come true.

—Fred Rogers
*children's television host*

# With the new day comes new strength.

—Eleanor Roosevelt
*humanitarian*

Some days there won't be a song in your heart. Sing anyway.

—Emory Austin
*motivational speaker*

Seeds of faith are always within us; sometimes it takes a crisis to nourish and encourage their growth.

—Susan L. Taylor
*editor*

# Everything passes if you learn to hold things lightly.

—Oprah Winfrey
*media mogul*

Our happiness or our unhappiness depends far more on the way we meet the events of life than on the nature of those events themselves.

—Wilhelm Von Humboldt
*philosopher*

There is no order in the world around us, we must adapt ourselves to the requirements of chaos instead.

—Kurt Vonnegut
*writer*

Right in the difficult we must have our joys, our happiness, our dreams: There against the depths of this background, they stand out, there for the first time we see how beautiful they are.

—Rainer Maria Rilke
*writer*

Even if happiness forgets you a little bit, never completely forget about it.

—Jacques Prevert
*writer*

To be hopeful, to embrace one possibility after another — that is surely the basic instinct . . . crying out: High tide! Time to move out into the glorious debris. Time to take this life for what it is!

—Barbara Kingsolver
*writer*

# Nothing can bring you peace but yourself.

—Ralph Waldo Emerson
*essayist/philosopher*

We can be unhappy about many things, but joy can still be there . . . It is important to become aware that at every moment of our life we have an opportunity to choose joy . . . It is in the choice that our true freedom lies, and that freedom is, in the final analysis, the freedom to love.

—Henri J.M. Nouwen
*theologian*

When we are unable to find tranquility within ourselves, it is useless to seek it elsewhere.

—Francois de La Rochefoucauld
*writer*

# Out of difficulties grow miracles.

—Jean de la Bruyere
*philosopher*

There is an alchemy in sorrow. It can be transmuted into wisdom, which, if it does not bring joy, can yet bring happiness.

—Pearl S. Buck
*writer*

# I breathe in and know that good things will happen.

—Tao Porchon-Lynch
*yoga master/author*

Hope is definitely not the same thing as optimism. It is not the conviction that something will turn out well, but the certainty that something makes sense, regardless of how it turns out.

—Vaclav Havel
*statesman*

Come from a space of peace and you'll find that you can deal with anything.

—Michael Singer
*businessperson/writer*

There's always going to be bad stuff out there. But here's the amazing thing -- light trumps darkness, every time. You stick a candle into the dark, but you can't still the dark into the light.

—Jodi Picoult
*writer*

But we can't live in the light all of the time. You have to take whatever light you can hold into the dark with you.

—Libba Bray
*writer*

# Take little bites of bravery.

—Lady Gaga
*singer*

Details aren't important no matter who asks, what, or how, or why. It's whether we stick the landing. To me, the ending is all that matters. And old love, we made it. We are on the other side. We are okay.

—Cristin O'Keefe Aptowicz
*writer*

The sky's changeups are reminders that this will not drag on forever.

—Monica de la Torre
*poet*

[C]ourage can be contagious, and hope can take on a life of its own.

—Michelle Obama
*attorney*

If you can't laugh when things go bad —laugh and put on a little carnival — then you're either dead or wishing you were.

—Stephen King
*writer*

On some dimension or other, every event in life can be causing only one of two things: either it is good for you, or it is bringing up what you need to look at in order to create good for you. Evolution is win-win . . . life is self-correcting.

—Deepak Chopra
*physician*

Promise me you will not spend so much time treading water and trying to keep your head above the waves that you forget, truly forget, how much you have always loved to swim.

> —Tyler Knott Gregson
> *poet*

How are we going to get through this craziness?" I asked. There was silence for a moment. "Left foot, right foot, left foot, breathe," he said.

—Anne Lamott
*writer*

Never be ashamed of how you feel. You have the right to feel any emotion you want and do what makes you happy.

—Demi Lovato
*singer*

You can't calm the storm, so stop trying. What you can do is calm yourself. The storm will pass.

—Timber Hawkeye
*writer*

You have dealt with so much, and done the best that you can. So, take a moment now to appreciate how strong you are.

—Karen Salmansohn
*artist/writer*

I often think I can't do this anymore but then I realize what choice do I have?

—Justin Blaney
*writer*

To be happy at any one point we must have suffered at the same. Never to suffer would have been never to have been blessed.

—Edgar Allen Poe
*writer*

If the road is easy, you're likely going the wrong way.

—Terry Goodkind

*writer*

Let's face it. You become a deeper person amidst adversity. You become a more perceptive, strong, resilient person when life is not handed to you on a silver platter held by a butler.

—Cathy Lamb
*writer*

Even from a dark night, songs of beauty can be born.

—Mary Anne Radmacher
*writer/artist*

Sweet are the uses of adversity
Which, like the toad, ugly and venomous,
Wears yet a precious jewel in his head.

—William Shakespeare
*writer*

We face up to awful things because we can't go around them, or forget them. The sooner you say "Yes, it happened, and there's nothing I can do about it," the sooner you can get on with your own life. You've got children to bring up. So you've got to get over it. What we have to get over, somehow we do. Even the worst things.

—Annie Proulx
*writer*

If you're in pitch blackness, all you can do is sit tight until your eyes get used to the dark.

—Haruki Murakami
*writer*

The best thing about your life is that it is in a constant state of design. That means you have, at all times, the power to redesign it.

—Cleo Wade
*poet*

Recognize that on certain days the greatest grace is that the day is over and you get to close your eyes. Tomorrow comes more brightly.

—Mary Anne Radmacher
*writer*

When we are no longer able to change a situation, we are challenged to change ourselves.

—Viktor Frankl
*psychiatrist*

Dear Stress, I would like a divorce. Please understand it is not you, it is me.

—Thomas E. Rojo Aubrey
*therapist/professor*

Extraordinary people survive under the most terrible circumstances and they become more extraordinary because of it.

—Robertson Davies
*writer*

# Who the hell said you no longer had it in you?

—Charles Bukowski
*writer*

You might not be aware of it, but you're full of light. Please, no matter how dark it gets, don't let the world dim you.

—Maxwell Diawuoh
*poet*

I can't prevent storms from coming, but I can decide not to invent my own.

—Emily P. Freeman
*writer*

Sometimes the most important thing in a whole day is the rest we take between two deep breaths.

—Etty Hillesum
*writer*

When you're lost in those woods, it sometimes takes you a while to realize that you are lost. For the longest time, you can convince yourself that you've just wandered off the path, that you'll find your way back to the trailhead any moment now. Then night falls again and again, and you still have no idea where you are, and it's time to admit that you have bewildered yourself so far off the path that you don't

even know from which
direction the sun rises
anymore.

—Elizabeth Gilbert
*writer*

The darker the night, the brighter the stars,
The deeper the grief, the closer is God!

—Fyodor Dostoevsky
*writer*

Trust yourself. You've survived a lot, and you'll survive whatever is coming.

—Robert Tew
*writer*

Keep walking through the storm. Your rainbow is waiting on the other side.

—Heather Stillufsen
*artist/writer*

# It's not time to worry yet.

—Harper Lee
*writer*

If today gets difficult,
remember ...
the smell of coffee
the way sunlight
bounces off a window
the sound of your
favorite person's
laugh
the feeling when a
song you love comes

on
the color of the sky at
dusk
and
that we are here to
take care of each
other.

—Nanea Hoffman
*writer*

Perhaps all anxiety might derive from a fixation on moments — an inability to accept life as ongoing,

—Sarah Manguso
*writer*

You can't stop the waves, but you can learn to surf.

—Jon Kabat-Zinn
*professor*

Hope smiles from the threshold of the year to come, whispering, "It will be happier."

—Alfred Lord Tennyson
*poet*

Resilience is very different than being numb. Resilience means you experience, you feel, you fail, you hurt. You fall. But, you keep going.

—Yasmin Mogahed
*scholar*

And remember: you must never, under any circumstances, despair. To hope and to act, these are our duties in misfortune.

—Boris Pasternak
*writer*

I've got some bad news and I've got some good news. Nothing lasts forever.

—Kate McGahan
*counselor/writer*

When you arise in the morning, think of what a precious privilege it is to be alive — to breathe, to think, to enjoy, to love.

—Marcus Aurelius
*emperor/philosopher*

# Do not lose heart. We were made for these times.

—Clarissa Pinkola Estes
*writer*

Everything will be okay in the end. If it's not okay, it's not the end.

—John Lennon
*musician*

,

Printed in Great Britain
by Amazon